PowerKiDS
Readers

SEA FRIENDS
LOS AMIGOS DEL MAR

WALRUSES
LAS MORSAS

SAM DRUMLIN
TRADUCCIÓN AL ESPAÑOL: EDUARDO ALAMÁN

PowerKiDS
press™

New York

Published in 2013 by The Rosen Publishing Group, Inc.
29 East 21st Street, New York, NY 10010

First Edition

Editor: Amelie von Zumbusch
Book Design: Liz Gloor and Colleen Bialecki   Traducción al español: Eduardo Alamán

Photo Credits: Cover Sue Flood/The Image Bank/Getty Images; pp. 5, 7, 24 iStockphoto/Thinkstock; p. 9 Wild Arctic Pictures/Shutterstock.com; p. 11 Hal Brindley/Shutterstock.com; p. 13 Paul Souders/Stone/Getty Images; p. 15 Jupiterimages/Photos.com/Thinkstock; p. 17 Leonard Lee Rue III/Photo Researchers/Getty Images; p. 19 Gail Johnson/Shutterstock.com; p. 21 Paul Nicklen/National Geographic/Getty Images; p. 23 Rodney Ungwiluk, Jr. Photography/Flickr/Getty Images.

Library of Congress Cataloging-in-Publication Data

Drumlin, Sam.
  [Walruses. English & Spanish]
  Walruses = Las morsas / by Sam Drumlin ; translated by Eduardo Alamán. — 1st ed.
      p. cm. — (Powerkids readers: sea friends = Los amigos del mar)
  Includes index.
  ISBN 978-1-4488-9977-7 (library binding)
  1. Walrus—Juvenile literature. I. Title. II. Title: Morsas.
  QL737.P62D7818 2013
  599.79'9—dc23
                                    2012022316

Web Sites: Due to the changing nature of Internet links, PowerKids Press has developed an online list of Web sites related to the subject of this book. This site is updated regularly. Please use this link to access the list: www.powerkidslinks.com/pkrsf/walrus/

Manufactured in the United States of America

CPSIA Compliance Information: Batch #W13PK3: For Further Information contact Rosen Publishing, New York, New York at 1-800-237-9932

CONTENTS

CONTENIDO

Walruses are big!

¡Las morsas son muy grandes!

They have fat called blubber.

Tienen una grasa parecida a la de las ballenas.

It keeps them warm.

_____

La grasa las mantiene
calientes.

They live in big herds.

Viven en grandes manadas.

Clams are their top food.

Las **almejas** son su principal alimento.

Females are cows.

A las morsas de sexo femenino se les llama hembras.

Males are bulls.

A las morsas de sexo masculino se les llama machos.

Bulls have longer **tusks**.

Los machos tienen **colmillos** más largos.

Most **calves** are born on the ice.

La mayoría de las **crías** nacen en el hielo.

They grow fast.

Crecen rápido.

~~RD TU K~~ /
PALABRAS QUE DEBES SABER

calf / (la) cría

clams /
(las) almejas

tusks /
(los) colmillos

INDEX

ÍNDICE